ACTUALLY.
BEST.
JOKES.
EVER.

JOKES for KIDS

CHANTELLE GRACE

BroadStreet
P U B L I S H I N G

BroadStreet Kids
Racine, Wisconsin, USA

BroadStreet Kids is an imprint of BroadStreet Publishing Group, LLC.
Broadstreetpublishing.com

ACTUALLY.BEST.JOKES.EVER.

ISBN 978-1-4245-5502-4
ISBN 978-1-4245-5547-5 (ebook)

Content compiled by Chantelle Grace.

Design by Chris Garborg | garborgdesign.com
Editorial services by Michelle Winger | literallyprecise.com

Printed in the United States of America.

17   18   19   20   21   22   23   7   6   5   4   3   2

Author Bio

CHANTELLE GRACE is a witty wordsmith who
loves music, art, and competitive games. She
is fascinated by God's intricate design of the
human body. As she works her way through
medical school, she knows it's important to
share the gift of laughter with those around
her. When she's not studying abroad, she
makes her home in Prior Lake, Minnesota.

TABLE OF CONTENTS ·····

KNOCK KNOCK JOKES

Knock, knock.

Who's there?

Cows go.

Cows go who?

No, cows go moo.

Knock, knock.

Who's there?

Mary.

Mary who?

Marry me?

Knock, knock.

Who's there?

Nerf.

Nerf who?

Your nephew.

Knock, knock.

Who's there?

Heart.

Heart who?

Heart to hear you. Can you speak up?

Knock, knock.

Who's there?

Honey.

Honey who?

Honey, I'm home.

Knock, knock.

Who's there?

Me.

Me, who?

You don't know who you are?

Knock, knock.

Who's there?

Ice cream.

Ice cream who?

Ice cream if you don't let me in.

Knock, knock.

Who's there?

Pecan.

Pecan who?

Pecan someone your own size.

Knock, knock.

Who's there?

Bison.

Bison who?

Bison girl scout cookies.

Knock, knock.

Who's there?

Water.

Water who?

Water way to answer the door.

Knock, knock.

Who's there?

Figs.

Figs who?

Figs the doorbell, it's broken.

Knock, knock.

Who's there?

Pudding.

Pudding who?

Pudding your shoes on before your pants is a silly idea.

Knock, knock.

Who's there?

Ketchup.

Ketchup who?

Ketchup to me and I will tell you.

Knock, knock.

Who's there?

Orange.

Orange who?

*Orange you going to answer
the door?*

Knock, knock.

Who's there?

Beets.

Beets who?

Beets me.

Knock, knock.

Who's there?

Water.

Water who?

*Water those plants
or they're going to die.*

Knock, knock.

Who's there?

Closure.

Closure who?

*Closure mouth while
you're eating, please.*

Knock, knock.

Who's there?

Sultan.

Sultan who?

Sultan pepper.

Knock, knock.

Who's there?

Two fours.

Two fours who?

No need to make lunch we already 8.

Knock, knock.

Who's there?

Imani.

Imani who?

Imani pickle, open the door.

Knock, knock.

Who's there?

Sweden.

Sweden who?

*Sweden the coffee
and open the door.*

Knock, knock.

Who's there?

Muffin.

Muffin who?

Muffin the matter with me, how about you?

Knock, knock.

Who's there?

Turnip.

Turnip who?

Turnip the volume, it's my favorite song.

Knock, knock.

Who's there?

Lettuce.

Lettuce who?

Lettuce in; it's cold.

Knock, knock.

Who's there?

Olive.

Olive who?

Olive you.

Knock, knock.

Who's there?

Omelet.

Omelet who?

Omelet smarter than I look.

Knock, knock.

Who's there?

Doughnut.

Doughnut who?

Doughnut disturb me.

Knock, knock.

Who's there?

Cash.

Cash who?

No thanks, but I'd like some peanuts.

Knock, knock.

Who's there?

Leaf.

Leaf who?

Leaf me alone.

Knock, knock.

Who's there?

Candy.

Candy who?

Candy cow jump over the moon?

Knock, knock.

Who's there?

Carrot.

Carrot who?

Do you even carrot all?

Knock, knock.

Who's there?

Celery.

Celery who?

Celery isn't high enough. I quit.

Knock, knock.

Who's there?

Pasta.

Pasta who?

Pasta la vista baby.

Knock, knock.

Who's there?

Eggs.

Eggs who?

Eggcited to meet you.

Knock, knock.

Who's there?

Broccoli.

Broccoli who?

*Broccoli doesn't have
a last name, silly.*

Knock, knock.

Who's there?

Noah.

Noah who?

Noah good place to eat?

Knock, knock.

Who's there?

Cook.

Cook who?

Hey, I'm not crazy.

Knock, knock.

Who's there?

Isma.

Isma who?

Isma lunch ready yet?

Knock, knock.

Who's there?

Butter.

Butter who?

*Butter tell you a few more
knock knock jokes.*

Knock, knock.

Who's there?

Stopwatch.

Stopwatch who?

*Stopwatch your doing
and open the door.*

Knock, knock.

Who's there?

Wire.

Wire who?

Wire you asking; I just told you.

Knock, knock.

Who's there?

Cotton.

Cotton who?

Cotton a trap, can you help me out?

Knock, knock.

Who's there?

See.

See who?

See you, if you'll let me in.

Knock, knock.

Who's there?

Alexia.

Alexia who?

Alexia again to open this door.

Knock, knock.

Who's there?

Toby.

Toby who?

*Toby or not Toby;
that is the question.*

Knock, knock.

Who's there?

Abby.

Abby who?

Abby birthday to you.

Knock, knock.

Who's there?

Adolph.

Adolph who?

Adolph ball hit me in the mouth.

Knock, knock.

Who's there?

Aida.

Aida who?

*Aida lot of sweets
and now I've got tummy ache.*

Knock, knock.

Who's there?

Al.

Al who?

*Al give you a hug
if you open this door.*

Knock, knock.

Who's there?

Aladdin.

Aladdin who?

*Aladdin the street wants
a word with you.*

Knock, knock.

Who's there?

Aldo.

Aldo who?

Aldo anywhere with you.

Knock, knock.

Who's there?

Alec.

Alec who?

Alec-tricity. Isn't that a shock?

Knock, knock.

Who's there?

Alex.

Alex who?

Alex-plain later; let me in!

Knock, knock.

Who's there?

Anna.

Anna who?

Anna going to tell you.

Knock, knock.

Who's there?

Ash.

Ash who?

*Bless you. I did not mean
to make you sneeze.*

Knock, knock.

Who's there?

Avery.

Avery who?

Avery thing but the kitchen sink.

Knock, knock.

Who's there?

Justin.

Justin who?

Just in time for dinner.

Knock, knock.

Who's there?

Rita.

Rita who?

Rita a little more and you'll find out.

Knock, knock.

Who's there?

Owl.

Owl who?

Owl aboard.

Knock, knock.

Who's there?

Chimp.

Chimp who?

I think it's pronounced shampoo.

WELL THAT'S PUNNY

Pencils could be made with erasers at both ends...

but what would be the point?

I was struggling to figure out how lightning works...

then it struck me.

She broke her finger today...

but on the other hand she was completely fine.

I've just been on a once-in-a-lifetime holiday.

I'll tell you what, never again.

I often say to myself...

"I can't believe that cloning machine worked!"

Some people say I'm addicted to somersaults...

but that's just how I roll.

Never lie to an x-ray technician.

They can see right through you.

My friend made a joke about a TV controller.

It wasn't remotely funny.

I have a speed bump phobia...

but I'm slowly getting over it.

I'm working on a device that will read minds.

I'd love to hear your thoughts.

I saw an ad that read: Television for free, volume stuck on full.

I thought to myself, I can't turn that down.

I thought about becoming a wizard...

so I tried it for a spell.

I got one of those new corduroy pillows.

They are making headlines.

I went to a restaurant last night and had the Wookie steak.

It was a little Chewy.

I have some broken puppets for sale.

No strings attached.

When it came to getting even with my local bus company...

I pulled out all the stops.

I find the best way to communicate with fish...

is to drop them a line.

My friend's bakery burned down last night.

Now his business is toast.

A man just hit me with milk,
cream, and butter.

How dairy.

I used to have a fear of hurdles...

but I got over it.

Inspecting mirrors is a job I could...

really see myself doing.

Someone just stole my mood ring.

I'm not sure how I feel about that.

Yesterday, I accidentally swallowed
some food coloring.

The doctor says I'm okay...
but I feel like I've dyed a little inside.

I never trust atoms.

They make up everything.

I get paid to sleep.

It's a dream job.

I can't believe I got fired from the calendar factory.

All I did was take a day off.

I was going to buy a book on phobias...

but I was afraid it wouldn't help me.

I can hear music coming out of my printer.

I think the paper's jammin' again.

It's really difficult to find what you want on eBay.

> *I was searching for fire starters and found over 15,000 matches.*

I don't trust these stairs...

> *they're always up to something.*

I had a neck brace fitted years ago.

> *I've never looked back since.*

My time machine and I...

> *go way back.*

My fear of moving stairs...

> *is escalating.*

Wind turbines.

I'm a big fan.

I used to be a train driver...

but I got sidetracked.

I left my friend because she wouldn't stop counting.

I wonder what she's up to now.

My sister bet me $100 that I couldn't build a working car out of spaghetti.

You should've seen her face as I drove pasta.

I did a theatrical performance about puns.

Really it was just a play on words.

My mom just found out that I replaced her bed with a trampoline.

She hit the roof.

Singing in the shower is all fun and games until you get shampoo in your mouth.

Then it becomes a soap opera.

I know how batteries feel.

I'm not included in most things either.

I heard a funny joke about a boomerang earlier.

I'm sure it'll come back to me eventually.

I asked the lion in my wardrobe what he was doing there;

he said it was "Narnia Business."

I tried to catch some fog.

I mist.

I knew a couple who met in a
revolving door.

*I think they're still
going around together.*

I woke up this morning and forgot
which side the sun rises from.

Then it dawned on me.

I'm very good friends with 25 letters
of the alphabet.

I don't know y.

DID YOU KNOW...

Jokes about German sausages
are the wurst.

The person who invented the door
knock won the No-bell prize.

Taller people sleep longer in a bed?

A golf ball is a golf ball no matter how
you putt it.

Never give your uncle an anteater.

Regular visitors to the dentist are familiar with the drill.

Reading while sunbathing makes you well red.

A chicken crossing the road is poultry in motion.

Claustrophobic people are more productive thinking outside of the box.

Whiteboards are remarkable.

Insect puns bug people.

Shout out to everyone wondering what the opposite of "in" is.

Time flies like an arrow. Fruit flies like a banana.

Two antennas met, fell in love, and eventually got married.

The wedding ceremony wasn't much, but the reception was excellent.

A small boy swallowed some coins and was taken to the hospital.
When his grandmother telephoned to ask how he was, the nurse said,

"No change yet."

Did you hear about the guy who got hit in the head with a can of soda?

He was lucky it was a soft drink.

Did you hear about the girl whose whole left side was missing?

She's all right now.

TRICKY TITLES

I Win

    by U. Lose

Robots

    by Anne Droid

Danger!

    by Luke Out

Cloning

    by Irma Dubble II

Hot Dog

by Frank Furter

I'm Fine

by Howard Yu

I'm Smarter

by Gene Yuss

Downpour

by Wayne Dwops

Sea Birds

by Al Batross

Teach Me

by I. Wanda Know

I Say So

by Frank O. Pinion

Tug of War

by Paul Harder

Surprised

by Omar Goodness

Good Works

by Ben Evolent

April Fools

by Sue Prize

Come On In

by Doris Open

Parachuting

    by Hugo First

Get Moving!

    by Sheik Aleg

I Like Fish

    by Ann Chovie

May Flowers

    by April Showers

Pain Relief

    by Ann L. Gesick

It's Unfair

    by Y. Me

How to Annoy
    by Aunt Agonize

40-Love
    by Dennis Court

The Roof Has a Hole
    by Lee King

African Safari
    by L.A. Funt

Ten Years in the Bathtub
    by Ima Prune

I Don't Smell Good
    by Anita Bath

The Art of Being Discreet
by Anonymous

101 Ways to Diet
by I. M. Hungry

Green Vegetables
by Broke Ali

Don't Raise Your Arms
by Harry Pitts

Sitting on the Beach
by Sandy Bottom

Window Coverings
by Kurt and Rod

How to Get Good Grades
　　by Samar T. Pants

The Skyline
　　by Bill Ding

Ouch!
　　by A. B. Sting

Helping Out
　　by Abel N. Willing

I Love You!
　　By Alma Heart

It Blew Off My Hat
　　by Augusta Wind

I Shoot Arrows
by Anne Archer

Not Optional
by Amanda Tory

Not A Cello
by Amanda Linn

What's for Dinner?
by Amelia Eat

Types of Birds
by A. V. Airy

How to Make Honey
by A. Beeman

Who Killed the Woodpecker?
by B. B. Gunn

How to Make Money
by Mell Yenere

Lucky As Can Be
by Bess Twishes

Sandwiches
by B. L. Tea

I Always Smell
by B. O. Issues

Stay Away
by Barb Dwire

Top Signs

by Bill Board

Let's Grill

by Barb E. Que

Fun Party Ideas

by Bobby Frapples

Haircuts

by Buz Cutt

Feelings

by Cara Lot

Suppertime

by Cam N. Getit

Dinosaurs that Eat Meat
   by Carn E. Vores

Lovely Jewels
   by Cristal Myne

How to Cook Bacon
   by Chris P. Swine

Music for Children
   by Zy L'fon

Rocket Launching
   by Leif Toff

Poor Sportsmanship
   by Collet Quits

A Day off Work
   by Collin Sic

Explaining it All
   by Clara Fye

Highway Travel
   by Dusty Rhodes

Plumbing Trouble
   by Dwayne Clog

White Flakes
   by Dan Druff

Tanned Legs
   by Denise R. Brown

Mosquitos

    by Drew Blood

Chores

    by Dustin Klean

Twelve Months

    by Dee Cember

Making Decisions

    by D. Side

Rats in the House

    by E. E. K. Mouse

Make Money Fast

    by E. Z. Cashe

Fun in the Sky
　　by Ella Copter

Drawing Tips
　　by Illis Traight

Full Tires
　　by Erin Side

She Sees Him
　　by Esau Hurr

Framed
　　by Gil T.

Pop History
　　by Ginger Ale

After Work
by Gwen Hom

Rapunzel Stories
by Harris Long

No Camels in the Zoo
by Humphrey Space

Delicious Breakfast Foods
by Hamm N. Eggs

Vegetarian Dinosaurs
by Herb A. Vore

His Girl Thursday
by Herman Friday

Funny People
by Hillary Uss

Baseball Tips
by Homer Run

Being a Jockey
by Hors Ryder

Need for a Recipe
by Ingrid E. Ants

The Post Office
by Imelda Letter

Planning a Surprise
by Izzy Backyet

The First Month
   by Jan Yuary

Lots of Colors
   by Jason Rainbows

How Airplanes Run
   by Jett Fuel

Where to Work Out
   by Jim Nasium

Don't Stop Believing
   by Kerry Onn

We're Almost There
   by Knot Quite

Honest People

> by Laura Byder

Ballet

> by Leah Tard

Help Out

> by Linda Hand

It's Fall

> by Leif Raker

Don't Be Greedy

> by Les Ismoore

Hawaiian Parties

> by Lou Wow

Speak Up

    by Louden Clear

We're Not All Winners

    by Lou Zer

How to Behave

    by B. Morell

Kings and Queens Rule

    by M. Pyres

The Perfect Ingredient

    by May O'Naze

The Best Thing on Pancakes

    by Mable Syrup

Favorite Dinners for Kids
by Mack Aroni

Computer Won't Work
by Mel Function

All in Your Head
by Mag Ination

Failing Classes
by Milo Grades

Where to Park a Boat
by Marina Dock

Not Brand New
by Mark Dupp

Karate

by Marsha Larts

Fire Me Up

by Matt Chez

Works of God

by Mira Q. Luss

You're Silly

by Noah Fence

The Flood

by Noah S. Arc

Playing Bridge

by Paco Cards

How to Read a Book
　　by Paige Turner

On a Budget
　　by Penny Pincher

ROFL RIDDLES

A king, queen, and twins are in a room.

How are there no people in the room?

They are beds.

A mirror for the famous, but informative to all. I'll show you the world, but it might be a bit small.

What am I?

A television.

How can you throw a ball 20 feet and have it come back to you without hitting anything?

Throw it up in the air.

What three positive numbers equal the same number when added or multiplied together?

1, 2, and 3.

There is a stone stove and a brick stove. You only have one match.

What do you light up first?

The match.

I have no wallet, but I pay my way.
I travel the world, but in the corner I stay.

What am I?

A stamp.

If you have three apples in one hand, and four apples in the other hand, what do you have?

Very large hands.

Jack's mother has three kids. April is the first one. May is the second child.

What's the third child's name?

Jack.

The dirtier I am, the whiter I get. You leave a mark on me when you stand, and I'll leave a mark on you when you sit.

What am I?

A chalkboard.

What occurs once in a minute, twice in a moment, but never in a thousand years?

The letter M.

You use me from your head to your toes; the more you use me the thinner I grow.

What am I?

A bar of soap.

What starts with e, but only has one letter in it?

An envelope.

When you need me, you throw me away. When you don't, you bring me back.

What am I?

An anchor.

What has to be broken before you can use it?

An egg.

What is the easiest way to poke a balloon without popping it?

Do it when it's not blown up.

I have every color, but no gold.

What am I?

A rainbow.

What is as old as the earth, but new every month?

The moon.

I fly, but I have no wings. I cry, but I have no eyes.

What am I?

A cloud.

Poor people have it. Rich people need it. If you eat it you die.

What is it?

Nothing.

100 feet in the air, but its back is on the ground.

What is it?

A centipede.

How do you make the number one disappear?

Add a g to it, and it's gone.

If you're in third place and you pass the person in second, what place are you in?

Second place!

Give me food and I will live, feed me water and I'll die.

What am I?

A fire.

The blue man lives in the blue house.
The green man lives in the green house.

Who lives in the white house?

The president.

I'm tall when I'm young, and I'm short when I'm old.

What am I?

A candle.

What starts with the letter T, is filled with T, and ends with the letter T?

A teapot.

There are three apples and you take away two.

How many apples do you have?

You took two, so of course you have two.

A boy fell off a 30-foot ladder, but didn't get hurt.

How is this possible?

He only fell off the first step.

I am an odd number, take away one letter and I become even.

What number am I?

> *Seven. If you take away the s, seven becomes even.*

The more you take, the more you leave behind.

What are they?

> *Footprints.*

A seven-letter word, with thousands of letters.

What is it?

> *Mailbox.*

Imagine you're in a room with no windows or doors and it's filling with water.

What do you do?

> *Stop imagining.*

At night they appear, but during the day they're lost.

What are they?

Stars.

What is black when you buy it, red when you use it, and gray when you throw it away?

Charcoal.

What is the best way to stop a dog from digging holes in the front yard?

Put it in the backyard.

What's the easiest way to double your money?

Hold it in front of the mirror.

What can be broken without being held?

A promise.

If an electric train is going south, which way is the smoke blowing?

An electric train doesn't have any smoke.

How can a pants pocket be empty and still have something in it?

It can have a hole in it.

What belongs to you, but others use it more than you do?

Your name.

A rooster lays an egg at six in the morning.

When does the farmer find it?

Never. A rooster doesn't lay eggs.

How many eggs can you put in an empty basket?

> *Only one, because after that, it's not empty.*

What's the longest word in the dictionary?

> *Smiles, because there's a mile between each S.*

If you look at my face, there won't be thirteen in any place.

What am I?

> *A clock.*

Everyone has me, but can't get rid of me.

What am I?

> *A shadow.*

I'm heavy, but not backwards.

What am I?

The word "ton."

I'm so delicate that even talking about me ruins me.

What am I?

Silence.

I brighten your day,
but I live in the shade.

What am I?

A lamp.

What word looks the same backwards and upside down?

Swims.

Who gets paid when they drive away their customers?

A taxi driver.

How many letters are in the alphabet?

There are eleven letters in "the alphabet."

A man shaves many times in one day, but still has a very long beard.

How does this happen?

He is a barber.

What's always coming, but never arrives?

Tomorrow.

I don't eat food, but I enjoy a light meal every day.

What am I?

A plant.

The more you take,
the more you leave behind.

What are they?

Stairs.

I run around the house,
but I don't move.

What am I?

A fence.

I have 88 keys, but can't open a door.

What am I?

A piano.

I have a foot but no leg.

What am I?

A ruler.

I'm round at the ends
and high in the middle.

What am I?

Ohio.

I have three letters and start with gas.

What am I?

A car.

I have a hand and fingers
but I am not alive.

What am I?

A glove.

I can run but I cannot walk.

What am I?

A drop of water.

I never ask questions
but often get answered.

What am I?

   A doorbell.

I can be caught but not thrown.

What am I?

   A cold.

I have three feet but cannot walk.

What am I?

   A yard stick.

TASTY TONGUE TWISTERS

I saw a saw that could out saw
any other saw I ever saw.

A big bug bit the little beetle but
the little beetle bit the big bug back.

Six slippery snails, slid slowly seaward.

How much wood could a wood chuck
chuck if a wood chuck could chuck wood.

Any noise annoys an oyster but
a noisy noise annoys an oyster more.

Fuzzy wuzzy was a bear.
Fuzzy wuzzy had no hair.
Fuzzy wuzzy wasn't fuzzy... was he?

If a black bug bleeds black blood,
what color blood does a blue bug bleed?

Crisp crusts crackle and crunch.

Round the rugged rocks
the ragged rascals ran.

Growing gray goats graze great green
grassy groves.

Which wrist watches
are Swiss wrist watches?

Fred fed Ted bread
and Ted fed Fred bread.

I scream, you scream,
we all scream for ice cream.

Four furious friends fought for the phone.

The cat catchers can't catch caught cats.

Three fluffy feathers fell from Fanny's flimsy fan.

Rory's lawn rake rarely rakes really right.

Toy boat. Toy boat. Toy boat.

She should shun the shining sun.

Cooks cook cupcakes quickly.

She sold six shabby sheared sheep.

Mix a box of mixed biscuits with a boxed biscuit mixer.

Twelve twins twirled twelve twigs.

If you notice this notice, you will notice
that this notice is not worth noticing.

The bottom of the butter bucket
is the buttered bucket bottom.

Five frantic frogs fled
from fifty fierce fish.

Betty and Bob brought back blue
balloons from the big bazaar.

Little Lillian lets lazy lizards lie along
the lily pads.

Does your sport shop stock short
socks with spots?

Many mumbling mice are making merry
music in the moonlight.

The boot black brought
the black boot back.

A synonym for cinnamon is a cinnamon
synonym.

The great Greek grape growers grow
great Greek grapes.

No need to light a nightlight on a light
night like tonight.

Green glass globes glow greenly.

Clean clams crammed in clean cans.

A slimy snake slithered
down the sandy Sahara.

She sees cheese.

Bake big batches of bitter brown bread.

Six socks sit in a sink,
soaking in soap suds.

Shave a single shingle thin.

She sells sea shells by the sea shore.

Shun the sunshine.

I wish to wish the wish you wish to wish.

A flea and a fly in a flue.

Fred fried fresh fruit on Friday.

THE GREAT OUTDOORS

What happens when you throw a red rock into a blue sea?

It sinks.

What language does a billboard speak?

Sign language.

Does China have a 4th of July?

Yes, right after the 3rd of July.

What is at the end of the rainbow?

The letter "w."

What kind of tree is carried in your hand?

A palm tree.

What did the red light
say to the green light?

Don't look, I'm changing.

What's purple and 5,000 miles long?

The Grape Wall of China.

What do you get when you pour
cement on a burglar?

A hardened criminal.

What do you call a knight
who is afraid to fight?

Sir Render.

Why don't mountains catch colds?

They have snow caps!